MW00387820

Siberian Cats as Pets.

The Complete Owner's Guide

by

Elliott Lang

Published by IMB Publishing 2013

Copyright and Trademarks. This publication is Copyright 2013 by IMB Publishing. All products, publications, software and services mentioned and recommended in this publication are protected by trademarks. In such instance, all trademarks & copyright belong to the respective owners. All rights reserved. No part of this book may be reproduced or transferred in any form or by any means, graphic, electronic, or mechanical, including photocopying, recording, taping, or by any information storage retrieval system, without the written permission of the author. Pictures used in this book are either royalty free pictures bought from stock-photo websites or have the source mentioned underneath the picture. Disclaimer and Legal Notice. This product is not legal or medical advice and should not be interpreted in that manner. You need to do your own due-diligence to determine if the content of this product is right for you. The author and the affiliates of this product are not liable for any damages or losses associated with the content in this product. While every attempt has been made to verify the information shared in this publication, neither the author nor the affiliates assume any responsibility for errors, omissions or contrary interpretation of the subject matter herein. Any perceived slights to any specific person(s) or organization(s) are purely unintentional. We have no control over the nature, content and availability of the web sites listed in this book. The inclusion of any web site links does not necessarily imply a recommendation or endorse the views expressed within them. IMB Publishing takes no responsibility for, and will not be liable for, the websites being temporarily unavailable or being removed from the internet. The accuracy and completeness of information provided herein and opinions stated herein are not guaranteed or warranted to produce any particular results, and the advice and strategies, contained herein may not be suitable for every individual. The author shall not be liable for any loss incurred as a consequence of the use and application, directly or indirectly, of any information presented in this work. This publication is designed to provide information in regards to the subject matter covered. The information included in this book has been compiled to give an overview of Achilles tendonitis and detail some of the symptoms, treatments etc. that are available to people with this condition. It is not intended to give medical advice. For a firm diagnosis of your condition, and for a treatment plan suitable for you, you should consult your doctor or consultant. The writer of this book and the publisher are not responsible for any damages or negative consequences following any of the treatments or methods highlighted in this book. Website links are for informational purposes and should not be seen as a personal endorsement; the same applies to the products detailed in this book. The reader should also be aware that although the web links included were correct at the time of writing, they may become out of date in the future.

Acknowledgements

Thanks to my husband and children for appreciating what I do and letting me do it.

To all the Siberian Cat owners I spoke to: thank you for your time and information.

4

Table of Contents

Table of Contents

Chapter 1. Introduction

Affectionate, playful and intelligent – if you are looking for a large breed of cat that will fill your days with enjoyment, then look no further than the Siberian Cat.

Known also as the Siberian Forest Cat, this breed is the official cat of Russia. They are a fairly new breed that was developed in the 1940's to 1950's but it wasn't until the 1980's that the breed was really established.

Despite its short history, the Siberian Cat is taking the cat world by storm. They are known for their amazing personality and calm nature that makes them perfect for any home. In addition, the breed is considered to be one of the largest breeds alive today with only the Maine Coon Cat beating them in overall size.

Still, even with that distinction, the Siberian Cat has an even bigger personality. This is a cat that loves to be with their owners and enjoys making them laugh. They are energetic yet calm, affectionate yet they aren't too clingy and they are a beautiful, semi-long haired cat that don't require a lot of grooming.

All in all, if you are looking for a perfect cat, you have found one in the Siberian Cat.

So if you are interested in learning more about this amazing breed, you have come to the right place.

Chapter 2. Snapshot of the Siberian Cat

Affectionate, playful and active are often three words used to describe this Russian cat breed. The Siberian Cat is a wonderful breed that I love in abundance. It can fit into any lifestyle and while it is an active breed, they love to sit and cuddle with their owners.

And although I can go over all the amazing traits of the Siberian Cat, I find that it is better to take a look at the breed in a quick snapshot, which is what this chapter is all about.

In this chapter, I will take you through what a Siberian Cat is specifically and also through the history and general facts of the breed.

1. What is a Siberian Cat?

The Siberian Cat, which is also known as the Siberian Forest Cat, is a breed of cat that was developed in Russia. The original breed was developed from stray cats that were brought into people's homes and domesticated.

While the breed was developed in the 1960's, there has been much evidence linking the breed to cats seen in Russia for centuries.

The Siberian Cat is considered to be one of the largest breeds of cats in the world. It is known by its semi-long coat, affectionate nature and energetic personality.

While it is still fairly unknown, the Siberian Cat is gaining some popularity throughout the world. It is the official cat of Russia and this title has led many to discover this wonderful breed.

2. History of the Siberian Cat

The Siberian Cat has a rather short history if you are looking at the breed specifically and not at the roots of the breed. It was developed in the 1980's officially; however, the breed is believed to have been developed sometime in the 1940's.

Originally, the Siberian Cat is believed to have started in the streets of Leningrad and other cities throughout Russia. Centuries ago, when Russia was overrun by rats, cats of varying breeds were imported into Russian cities to help catch the rats.

While the cats were imported for a purpose, the majority of cats in Russia became strays. They would find shelter and food on their own and often became adopted by families, which made them domesticated.

It is from these stray cats that the Siberian Cat was first developed and there is very little information on what breeds went into the creation of the breed.

The Siberian Cat was first developed in the 1960's and breeding began on a very small scale in Moscow and Leningrad. The breeders who developed the Siberian Cat created them from strays that they had domesticated.

During the 1970's, breeding of these cats slowed and it wasn't until the end of the 1980's that breeders returned to creating the Siberian Cat.

By 1987, a breed standard was created and registrations for the Siberian Cat began in St. Petersburg under the Kotofei Cat Club. Shortly after that time, the Fauna Club of Moscow began registering the breed.

Since then, efforts have been made to keep the Siberian Cat a purebred cat. These efforts continue with a breed standard and also with showing the breed to ensure breeders are educated about what a healthy Siberian Cat should look like.

While it is still fairly unknown, the Siberian Cat has been imported into Western Europe as well as North America where it is quickly gaining popularity.

3. General Facts about the Siberian Cat

Before we look at how to care for your Siberian Cat, it is important to be aware of some quick facts about the Siberian Cat. Later on in this book, I will go over temperament and other facts about the breed but these general facts will give you a good idea if the Siberian Cat is the right breed for you.

Is the Siberian Cat a wild cat?

The Siberian Cat is often called the Siberian Forest Cat and it is this name that often confuses people. While it was developed from stray cats in Russia, the cats were domesticated and were not actually wild cats.

It is important to note that there are breeders who claim that the Siberian Cat is wild in nature and comes from a small, wild cat; the theories on how it was developed link it directly with stray cats in Russia and you do not find the breed in the wild.

Do Siberian Cats make good pets?

Absolutely. Siberian Cats are friendly, affectionate and usually very active. They are very much a cat breed that can fit into any lifestyle and they are usually very easy to care for despite having a longer coat.

Are Siberian Cats good with children?

The answer is yes, without a doubt the Siberian Cat is excellent with children. They are usually very patient with children and will often seek them out for attention. That being said, if a child mishandles a Siberian Cat, it can become timid and even aggressive towards kids so it is important to teach children how to handle the cat.

Are they clean?

Cats, in general, are clean animals and will constantly groom themselves to maintain a clean coat. Siberian Cats are no different and are considered to be clean.

That being said, they do shed hair, however, they are considered to be low shedders with only two shedding periods in the year. In addition, all cats will have kitty litters, which can be quite messy, especially if they are not properly cleaned.

Can they live in any type of dwelling?

Yes, Siberian Cats can live in any type of dwelling and don't have many extra needs as a breed.

Are they noisy?

No, Siberian Cats are a quiet breed and while they will meow, they usually communicate with soft mews and chirps instead of through loud crying.

What is the lifespan of a Siberian Cat?

A Siberian Cat has a very long lifespan and it is not uncommon for them to reach the age of 12 to 14 years of age. Many live much longer than that and some can reach the age of 18.

Are they illegal to own?

Since Siberian Cats are not actually developed from wild breeds, they are not illegal to own. That being said, make sure you check with your own local bylaws to ensure that the Siberian Cat is not restricted.

How big do Siberian Cats get?

Siberian Cats are considered to be one of the biggest breeds of cats alive today. They usually average between 8 to 15 pounds and many can weigh more.

How long do they take to mature?

The Siberian Cat usually reaches sexual maturity at the age of 6 months for females and 10 months for males. However, they are not considered to be fully grown until they are 1 year of age.

Are Siberian Cats expensive to own?

In general, Siberian Cats are no more expensive to raise than other breeds of cats. There is the initial purchasing expense, however, when the Siberian Cat is an adult, its average cost of ownership is about 500USD or £300 per year. This equals roughly 40USD or £25 per month and includes food, yearly medical costs, toys and miscellaneous items a cat may need. During the first year of your Siberian Cat's life, the cost goes up slightly and can range from 650 to 800USD or £400 to £500. This is due to the added medical care necessary, paying for altering and the initial supplies that you need.

One thing that should be mentioned is that some breeders will sell their kittens altered, which means that they are already spayed or neutered. This means that those initial, first year costs are not as high for you but often the price of the kitten is at the higher end.

Do they cost a lot?

When you look at the cost of Siberian Cats compared to an average housecat you purchase from the newspaper, they can be quite expensive. On average, Siberian Cats cost around 900 to 1200 USD or £550 to £800. The price varies depending on the terms of the breeder and the area that they live in. In addition, many breeders spay or neuter their kittens before sale and the price often reflects this practice.

Should they be indoor pets?

While there is a big debate on whether a cat should be indoor or outdoor, Siberian Cats can thrive as both an indoor and outdoor cat. That being said, cats do much better as indoor and providing them with a safe enclosure outside is much better than allowing them to roam.

Are they good ratters?

Yes, Siberian Cats are active and this gives them the athleticism to be excellent ratters. In addition, since they have been developed from stray cats, the Siberian Cat still has many of the instinctual drives needed to be a good ratter.

Can they live in colder climates?

Siberian Cats do very well in colder climates since they have a long triple coat.

And there you have the general facts about the Siberian Cat. Now that you have some information on the breed, let's dive a little deeper and explore this truly amazing breed.

Chapter 3. Breed Standard of the Siberian Cat

Although I have gone over the snapshot of the Siberian Cat, I want to take a few moments to go over the breed standard for the Siberian Cat.

The main reason for this is that many people are not aware of the standard. In addition, since there is some miscommunication about the standard, there are many Siberian Cats sold that aren't true Siberian Cats. Being aware of the standard will help you steer clear of scams.

The breed standard that I am using for this book is the breed standard by the Cat Fancier's Association (CFA). The breed can be registered with the CFA as well as with the following organizations:

* The International Cat Association (TICA)
* Fèdèration International Fèline (Fife)
* World Cat Federation (WCF)
* Governing Council of the Cat Fancy *(GCCF)*

We will be going through each area of the cat to give you an idea of what the Siberian Cat breed standard should be.

1. Head

The head includes the neck, nose, eyes, ears, cheeks, jaw and forehead in the breed standard. The main points with the breed standard head are:

The head should be massive in size. It should be slightly rounded with a slightly longer than broad proportion. The neck of the

18

Siberian Cat should be medium in length. It should be well muscled and should be in proportion to the body.

The forehead of the Siberian Cat should be broad with a slight indentation. There should be no stop between the forehead and nose and the nose itself should be medium in length and broadness.

The Siberian Cat should have a well-shaped face with a chin that has a slight slope when you look in profile. In addition, the jaw should be wide but gently rounded and should look strong. The cheeks should be round and set high on the face.

The ears should be medium in length with a slightly rounded tip. They should sit on the head with a good width between them and should tilt forward slightly.

The eyes of the Siberian Cat should be set wide apart and they should have a slightly oblique look to them. While the large, slightly oval shaped eyes can be any colour, green is the preferred colour according to breed standards.

2. Body

When we are referring to the body of the Siberian Cat, we are also looking at the legs, paws and tail of the cat as well as the main body.

In general, the Siberian Cat should have a well-muscled body. It should be medium in length and should be slightly rectangular in proportion. Its length should be slightly longer than its height.

The build of the Siberian Cat should be one of a solid cat. They should have a broad chest and the body should be thick boned that gives them some weight.

The legs should be thick and strong and the paws should be large and in proportion to the rest of the body. The paws should be rounded and it should have tufts of fur between each toe. The cat itself should be medium height.

The tail of the Siberian Cat should be long and should be free of any kinks. It should be thick and should have a rounded tip. The tail should have a thick, dense coat covering it without appearing overly shaggy.

3. Coat

The coat of the Siberian Cat is one of the features that really identifies the breed from other breeds. While many cats have a double coat, the Siberian Cat should have a triple coat. The hairs should be equal length with a thick undercoat, which is usually thinner in the summer.

The hair length of the coat should be semi-long so the cat has a sculpted appearance. They should never look shaggy and the coat should never be as long as a Persian. The hair should have a water repellent topcoat that should be hard to the touch.

In addition, the coat should be glossy and there should be a distinct shirtfront on the coat as well as a full frill and britches. The hair on the belly and britches can curl; however, it should not be a thick curl. The tail and paws should be well coated and there should be tufts of fur between the toes.

4. Colour

The final area to look at with the breed standard is the colour of the Siberian Cat. In general, the Siberian Cat can be found in every colour and all colours are accepted. In addition, all patterning is accepted in the breed standard.

The only exception to the colour is cinnamon, chocolate, fawn and lilac. The breed standard does not recognize these colours, however, they have been seen in the breed. In addition, pointed patterns have not been accepted. Regardless of colour, white is accepted in any amount or on any location on the Siberian Cat.

Finally, the leather on the nose, paw pads and eye rims should match the colour of the cat.

5. Faults

Although faults are not something that really needs to be looked at for the average pet owner, if you are interested in breeding and showing your Siberian Cat, it is important to understand the faults in the breed. It is recommended that you avoid breeding cats with the faults to maintain the look and standard of the breed.

With the Siberian Cat, any fine boning or the cat appearing small with a light build is considered a fault. Long legs or a cat that is too short is also a fault. In addition, a short tail is considered a serious fault.

In addition, if the head is rounded and has a long, straight or narrow profile, the cat does not meet breed standard.

Eyes should not be round and the ears should not be large or set high on the head.

The coat is very important to breed standard and should never appear like a Persian coat. In addition, it should be full and should never be thin, except when it is summer.

And that is your Siberian Cat. As you can tell, the Siberian Cat should be a heavy cat with a strong build and broad head. They are quite noble looking and while they have a refined look, they are not overdone as to appear delicate.

Chapter 4. The Siberian Cat Personality

Although many breed standards call for certain personalities, I wanted to touch on the Siberian Cat's personality separately. The main reason for this is because these are truly exceptional cats that make owning a cat a complete joy.

They are known as being very affectionate and often, people are surprised by how affectionate a cat can be – considering that they are often viewed as an aloof roommate rather than an affectionate pet.

The Siberian Cat is anything but an elusive companion and they are always happy to be standing by your side. In fact, many people have found that the Siberian Cat is always trying to spend time with their owners.

What this means is that the cat is happy to trail after you and make sure that he is always by your side. Many owners have found that their Siberian Cat won't even let them go to the bathroom without being by their side.

In many ways, the Siberian Cat has a canine like temperament and they will often greet owners at the door. They also love to spend the evening after you get home sitting in your lap and quietly speaking to you.

Speech is another interesting trait of this breed. While they are not a loud breed, they often communicate with their owners through a range of noises. Siberian Cats are known for their soft mews, chirps, trills and purring. This is a breed that likes to speak with their owners and they will do so often.

Besides being an affectionate companion, the Siberian Cat is known as being an active one. This breed has a lot of energy and while it will rest throughout the day, it is also happy to be exploring the world around them.

In addition, the Siberian Cat is a very playful cat and while many breeds are shy of strangers, the Siberian Cat will play with everyone, including strangers.

The breed is known for being trainable and you can teach your Siberian Cat a range of tricks. They often love to play fetch and will learn a range of other tricks with ease.

In fact, training is a good way to keep your Siberian Cat out of trouble since the breed is so intelligent. Left to its own devices, a Siberian Cat will find ways to get into trouble and will often steal things such as jewellery. Keep plenty of toys on hand for your cat.

This is a working breed and it has a lot of athleticism because of this. You will often find your Siberian Cat climbing to the highest area in your home – including the tops of doors. If you have any rodents in or around your home, you will also have a few presents brought to you, as Siberian Cats are excellent ratters.

They do very well with other cats and animals and can often thrive in multi-cat and multi pet homes.

Another unique trait that the Siberian Cat has is its love of water. This is a breed that will play in water and will simply sit in a bathtub enjoying the warm waves. The breed, with the exception of a few cats, has no fear of water and this makes bathing so easy for owners.

Finally, the Siberian Cat is a versatile breed that does well in any type of home. They are calm enough to be therapy cats and will enjoy a quiet home but they are active enough not to be overwhelmed by a busy home.

They generally love children and will often seek them out if any are present in the home. Overall, this breed is well rounded and makes cat ownership a joy.

Chapter 5. Preparing for your Siberian Cat

As you have read, the Siberian Cat is a wonderful companion and if you are ready to add one to your home, it is important to prepare for it.

One of the hardest things to do with a Siberian Cat is to actually buy one. While they are gaining popularity and recognition as a breed, the Siberian Cat is still fairly unknown. What this means is that there are fewer breeders and fewer litters for you to choose a kitten from.

In addition to having difficulty locating a breeder, many breeders have long waiting lists and you can expect having to wait for a kitten. While you are waiting, you should begin preparing your home for a kitten.

In this chapter, we will go over everything you need to know in preparing for your Siberian Cat and will also take you through how to choose a breeder and where to find your very own Siberian Cat.

1. Supplies for your Cat

Although many people purchase a kitten on a spur of the moment and then rush out to purchase all the supplies, that is not something that I recommend that you do. Instead, it is important to plan for your cat and to purchase the supplies beforehand.

The supplies that you need for a Siberian Cat kitten is really no different than the supplies that you would need for any breed of kitten. In addition, you will need the same supplies whether you are purchasing a kitten or an adult Siberian Cat.

It is important to note that I have listed all of the essential supplies as well as all of the supplies that aren't really necessary. While you can purchase a lot of things for your kitten, don't feel that you have to. Owning a Siberian Cat shouldn't bankrupt you when you go and purchase the supplies.

a) Essential Supplies

These are items that I strongly recommend that you buy, regardless of the age of your cat.

1. Food and water dishes:

Choose food and water dishes for your kitten that are easy for your kitten to feed from. In addition, make sure they are easy to clean. I recommend ceramic bowls or stainless steel bowls, as they are cleaner. In addition, they do not harbour bacteria like plastic bowls will.

2. Bed:

While many people overlook a bed for their kitten, I find that it really helps with transitioning a kitten to their new home. While they are still young, your Siberian Cat will not be able to climb up onto furniture so having a soft bed to sleep on will make him feel comfortable and safe.

3. Litter Box:

A litter box is a must have item for your kitten. There are a number of different boxes and it is important to find one that works for your cat. Make sure that it is low enough for your kitten to get in and also check how your kitten reacts to it.

Litter boxes with lids can help keep the litter area clean, however, some kittens are scared of the litter box lid and will avoid using the kitty litter if it has one. In addition, electric kitty litter boxes can also be scary for kittens so don't rush out and purchase the latest and greatest in kitty litter appliances until you know your kitten's temperament.

When you are buying your litter box, don't forget to purchase the litter.

4. Collar:

Every kitten needs a collar in the event that he slips out the door. Since Siberian Cats are so energetic and inquisitive, it is very important for your kitten to have one.

In addition to the collar, make sure that you have an identification tag on the kitten. This should include your pet's name and your contact information including your name, address and telephone number.

5. Microchip

While some kittens are sold with a microchip, if your kitten is not, it is something I strongly recommend. Often, you can get micro chipping done for around £20UK or $20 to $35 in the US and it will see to the safety of your Siberian Cat since all of its information is on the microchip. If your cat happens to get out and a rescue picks him up, they will be able to contact you about your pet.

6. Cat Carrier

Another item that is often overlooked by cat owners is the carrier but I strongly recommend these. Cat carriers enable you to carry your cat from the vets, the groomers or anywhere else that you need to take your cat. It is a safe way to store your kitten and will help prevent it being insured during high stress situations.

When you purchase a cat carrier, purchase one for the size your cat is going to be and not the size that he is as a kitten. Having to replace the cat carrier as your kitten grows is a waste of money and not necessary.

7. Grooming Tools

While the Siberian Cat does not require a large amount of grooming, the semi-long coat will require some care. In addition, cats do require regular grooming care, regardless of their coat type. Before you bring home a Siberian Cat or kitten, make sure that you have the following grooming items:

* Slicker Brush
* Undercoat Brush
* Flea Comb
* Nail Clippers
* Toothbrush for cats
* Toothpaste for cats

And those are all the essentials that you will need for your cat.

b) Non-essential Supplies

Now that you know what the essential supplies are, it is time to look at the non-essential supplies. Non-essentials are just that, things that you don't necessarily need to have but they are still nice to have.

1. Toys:

Although toys could be considered an essential supply, it is not one that I recommend as an essential. Instead, you can buy toys as needed or not at all. If you don't have toys, however, be prepared for your Siberian Cat to find things of his own to play with, including your jewellery.

When you purchase a toy, make sure that they are safe for your cat. Avoid toys that have buttons or bells that can be chewed off and swallowed.

2. Harness:

If you plan on leash training your Siberian Cat, a harness is definitely something that you should purchase for your kitten. However, if you are not planning on training your kitten to a leash, then there is no reason to purchase a harness and you could go without.

3. Leash:

This is the same as the harness and is only needed if you are going to be training your Siberian Cat to a leash. Unlike some breeds, Siberian Cats train very easily to the leash and I would recommend it so that your cat can have some outdoor time without it becoming dangerous for your cat.

4. Outdoor Enclosure:

One item that has been gaining some popularity is an outside enclosure. These are enclosures that are usually accessed through a kitty door built in your home's wall. They are completely enclosed so the cat cannot wander away from the home but are made with wire so the cat can enjoy the outdoors.

While these are not a must have if you have a cat, Siberian Cats do enjoy going outside so I would recommend them. They give your cat the opportunity to really enjoy both the indoors and the outdoors without worrying about him escaping and running off.

5. Scratching Post:

I have had mixed results with scratching posts. Sometimes they work, sometimes they don't. Still, I would recommend purchasing a scratching post to prevent your Siberian Cat from scratching up your furniture.

And that is all you really need, except food. However, I will go over food in the chapter on feeding your Siberian Cat.

2. What to Look for in a Breeder

You have the supplies; you know that you want a Siberian Cat, now all you have to do is find one. Before you start looking through the pet ads, it is important to understand what to look for in a breeder before you go and meet one.

Later on in this chapter, I have listed a number of breeders and sites to get you started on your search, however, before you go over those lists, it is important to understand what to look for when you visit and talk with your breeder.

The very first thing that you should do is become familiar with the Siberian Cat breed. If you haven't done so already, read the chapters on breed standard and personality. Understanding the breed will give you a clear idea of what you want and if the breeder's cats fall into the breed standard. If they don't, avoid that breeder.

The next thing you should do is contact the breeder you are interested in. Take the time to review the breeder's website and also check out the breed clubs to find out if they are members in good standing.

Once you have done all the background work, contact the breeder through email or by telephone. I believe that a good rule of thumb to go by is how the breeder treats you when you are first getting into contact with them.

If the breeder is impolite or does not help you by answering questions, then it is better to look for a different breeder. Often, your first impression with a breeder is the correct impression.

If the breeder is polite, answers your questions and seems genuinely interested in you and the home that you will be providing a kitten, then it is usually a good indicator that you are speaking with an excellent breeder.

When you have made that first contact, be sure to let the breeder know what sex of kitten you would like, if you have a preference for colour or patterns and when you are looking to bring a kitten home. Although you may not be able to purchase a kitten from that breeder, most breeders network and he/she should be able to direct you to a breeder who will have kittens sooner.

While it may not be an option, if you are able to, visit the cattery where your kitten will be purchased. Always check to make sure that the cattery is clean and that the animals are healthy. Also make sure that they are being housed properly and are not covered in any parasites.

If you can't visit the cattery, which is often the case with Siberian Cats, ask to see photos of the cattery. You may not be able to see much but you can get some idea of what the cattery looks like from the photos.

Regardless of whether you visit a cattery or not, make sure you ask the breeder the following questions:

1. Are your kittens registered?

If you are looking for a pet quality kitten, the answer is usually that you don't need it to be registered. However, a registration paper will help ensure that you have purchased a purebred Siberian Cat. In addition, making sure that the breeder only breeds registered cats will give you better reassurance that you are purchasing a purebred Siberian Cat.

2. Do you have pedigrees?

This often goes hand in hand with registration but check to see if the breeder has pedigrees on all of their breeding cats. Also ask if the kittens will be sold with a pedigree.

It is important to note that Siberian Cats are still fairly new so the pedigree does not usually go back that far.

3. How do you raise your kittens?

This is a very important question, as how the kittens are raised will greatly affect how your Siberian Cat is both socially and physically. Make sure that the kittens are raised underfoot and in the home. If the kittens are raised in a cattery away from people, your kitten will be timid and shy and you won't get the temperament you want to see in your cat.

4. Are the parents available for viewing?

In some cases, the male cat will not be available for viewing simply because the breeder used a stud from another breeder. If that is the case, you should still be able to see photos of the male as well as his registration papers and his pedigree.

If the cats are at the cattery and you live close enough to travel to it, go and see the cats in person. Look at their size, temperament and health before deciding on the breeder. If the breeder will not allow you to view the parents, choose a different breeder.

5. Do you have references from kitten buyers?

Although every cattery has to start somewhere, if you find that a large, established cattery has no references to give you, then you should look elsewhere.

Catteries that have been established for years will have families who have purchased kittens from them. Reputable breeders will have references from past kitten owners.

One word of caution on references, however, most references will be good regardless of the breeder. The majority of breeders will not give you bad references so you should always take references with a grain of salt.

6. How many litters do you produce in a year?

This is a very important question because a breeder who produces more than 2 or 3 litters in a year is less likely to spend the time necessary to ensure the kittens are well taken care of and socialized.

Socialization is vital for Siberian Cat kittens and you want to choose a breeder that can give the kittens the majority of his/her attention.

7. What age do the kittens go home?

Another important question to ask is when the kittens go home. While many people think of 8 weeks as the age that kittens go to their new homes, it is actually later than that. You want to make sure that your breeder only sends the kittens home after 10 weeks of age.

Although kittens can start going home at 8 weeks of age, they benefit greatly from those last two weeks with their mom and will be a more well-rounded and better-socialized kitten.

8. Will a veterinarian examine the kittens?

A sign that the breeder is taking good care of her kittens is the veterinarian care that the kittens receive. Ask to find out if the kittens will be examined by a veterinarian and if they will have their first shots with the vet. If the answer is yes, see if the vet will provide the breeder with a health certificate.

9. Do you sell your kittens with a health guarantee?

The Siberian Cat is a fairly hardy breed that doesn't have a large number of genetic diseases, however, a sign of a good breeder is one that will give you a health guarantee in the event that your kitten develops a specific disease in the first year or two of life.

10. Will you ship your kittens?

Finally, check to find out if the breeder will ship his/her kittens and how much shipping is. Some breeders will only sell locally so it may lead to you needing to cross them off the list if you don't live close to them.

And that is about all you need to ask the breeder. Make sure you find out about the cost of a kitten. When you are speaking to the breeder, take the time to answer the breeder's questions. One indication that a breeder is a reputable breeder is the interest the breeder takes in you. If she doesn't talk to you about the home you will be providing for your kitten, then he/she probably isn't that reputable and the care of the kittens may be lacking.

After your phone conversations, if you have the opportunity to go and meet the breeder, look for the following points:

** Is the Cattery Clean?*

Always make sure that the cattery is clean. Check for faeces and urine, which you can smell very easily. If it is not clean, then you want to avoid that breeder.

On the other hand, if it is clean and sterile, you will probably want to look elsewhere too. Overly clean can indicate that the cats are raised in kennels with little human contact, which is something you do not want with your kitten.

** Does the Cattery have Space?*

Another thing to look at is whether the cattery has space for the cats there. Are they kept in kennels or do they get free roam of the cattery? While kennels are not always bad, they should have a minimum of 27 cubic feet per cat. If the cat doesn't have that room in their pen, then the cattery is too small and may indicate other problems.

* Are there Toys for the Cats?

Siberian Cats love to play and they need a lot of things to interact with. Observe the environment and take note of the number of toys, scratching posts and climbers that the cats have. The more you see, the more you know the breeder is investing in the well being of his/her cats.

* How does the Breeder Interact with the Cats?

Finally, watch how the breeder interacts with the cats. If he/she ignores them or mistreats them in any way, find a different breeder.

Once you have visited, you should feel confident about your breeder. If you don't at any time, choose a different breeder.

3. How to Choose a Kitten

So, you have chosen a breeder and there is a litter for you to choose your kitten from. It can be an exciting time and many people will often pick the first kitten that walks up to them. While this practice is okay, it isn't something that I recommend to you.

Often, the first kitten that walks up to a person is the kitten that is more energetic and inquisitive. It is not necessarily that the kitten is choosing you since that kitten may choose everyone that comes into the home. Instead, take the time to sit back and monitor the kittens at play.

Ask the advice of the breeder while you are watching them and find out the temperament of each one. Trust me, the breeder will have a lot of information on the temperaments of the kittens and will give you the information you need to make the right choice.

When you are observing the kitten, you want to look at the health of the kitten first. After you look at the health, you can decide which kitten to take based on colour, gender, pattern and temperament.

To do a quick health check, look for the following traits:

* *Activity Level*: The kitten should be playful and not lethargic. Even kittens at rest should not be drooping as they sleep.

* *Eyes:* Eyes are very important when assessing health and your kitten should have bright eyes that are free of any discharge. In addition, dangle your keys or wave a toy in front of them to determine if the kitten can see clearly.

* *Ears:* Ears should be free of debris and dirt and should have a healthy colour to them. In addition, make noises to see if the kitten can hear you easily or if there are signs of hearing problems.

* *No discharge:* There should be no discharge from the kitten's nostrils, mouth or eyes.

* *Healthy Mouth:* Take the time to open the kitten's mouth and look inside. Teeth should be properly aligned and there shouldn't be any broken or cracked teeth. Gums should be pink and healthy.

* *Good proportioned:* Judge the kitten according to the breed standard and make sure the proportions of the body are similar to the proportions set out in the breed standard.

___

* *Clean coat and skin:* Run your fingers through the fur to get a look at the skin. Make sure there is no dandruff or parasites and that the skin is clean and free of sores and rashes. The coat should be shiny.

* *Socialized:* Watch how the kitten reacts to stimuli in the home and how they react to you. Siberian Cats should be affectionate and very accepting of strangers. If your kitten doesn't warm up to you shortly after you come in, then it probably isn't the kitten for you.

And that is all you need to look at with regards to the kitten's health. If the kittens are healthy, simply choose according to your colour and gender preference.

4. Rescuing an Older Siberian Cat

Although much of this chapter has been on selecting your own kitten, a lot can be said about rescuing older cats. While it can be difficult to find an older Siberian Cat at a shelter since they are relatively unknown, adult cats can be found on pet ads and even from breeders.

In fact, it is very common for breeders to re home adult cats when the cat has reached the end of its breeding career. There are many benefits to adopting an older cat and these are:

* *First Year Expenses:* Often, the first year of expenses is covered with an older cat. The cat has been spayed or neutered and has all of his or her shots.

* *Established Temperament:* This can be a con as well but generally, you can see what the cat will be like as an adult when it is an adult.

* Adjusts into a Multi-pet Home Easier: Believe it or not, but older cats often do much better going into a multi-pet home than kittens. The reason for this is because older cats are not as high energy as younger cats and this causes less stress on the pets you already have.

* Slowed Down: While kittens can be cute, the high energy of a kitten can be trying at times. An older cat has outgrown the high level of mischievousness that kittens have.

As you can see, adopting an older Siberian Cat can have a lot of benefits. If you are planning on adopting an older cat, follow the same screening that you would do with a kitten. Make sure that you find out the history of the cat, how it does with other pets and people and get a health record. If everything is in order, bring home your older cat to enjoy.

5. Where to Find a Siberian Cat

Okay, now that you know what to look for in a breeder and kitten, it is time to get down to finding the Siberian Cat. As I have mentioned before, finding a Siberian Cat can be tricky business since the breed is still uncommon.

What this can mean is that when you are ready for a Siberian Cat, there may not be a litter ready for you. Many breeders have long waiting lists and it can be a wait of up to a year before you can bring home your kitten.

With that said, the first place that I always recommend that you start with is your local cat fancier associations. Many of them have lists of breeders according to breed and they will help you find the right breeder for you.

Cat associations to contact are:

41

* American Association of Cat Enthusiasts (AACE), www.aaceinc.org

* American Cat Fancier's Association (ACFA), www.acfacat.com

* Canadian Cat Association (CCA), www.cca-afc.com

* Cat Fanciers' Association (CFA), www.cfainc.org

* Cat Fanciers' Federation (CFF), www.cffinc.org

* National Cat Fanciers' Association (NCFA), www.nationalcatfanciers.com

* The International Cat Association (TICA), www.tica.org

* The Traditional Cat Association, Inc. (TCA), www.traditionalcats.com

a) Breed Clubs

If you can't find what you are looking for with regards to cat associations, I recommend that you try a breed club. There are fewer breed clubs for Siberian Cats than there are for other breeds; however, there are a few breed clubs established for this breed. They are:

* TAIGA Siberian Cat Breed Club: www.taigasiberianclub.com

* The Siberian Cat Club: www.siberian-cat-club.co.uk

* Siberian Cat World: www.siberiancatworld.org

b) Breeders

I have provided you with a list of breeders that you can purchase a Siberian Cat from. These breeders are all over the world and while this may not be a complete list, they will get you started.

One word of caution, I have never worked with any of these breeders so I am not sure how they are to work with. It is important to do proper research on all of the breeders and be to sure to follow the steps to choosing a breeder that I have laid out.

Breeders of Siberian Cats

* Sonshanley Siberian: www.sonshanleysiberiancats.com

* Miakoschka Siberian Cattery, www.siberiancats.com.au

* Snowgum Siberians: www.siberiankittens.com.au

* Silvercloud Siberian Cats: www.silvercloudsiberiancats.com

* Sibirela: www.sibirela.bravehost.com

* Purrshka Siberian Cats: purrshkasiberiancats.com

* Ontario Siberians: www.ontariosiberians.com

* Iceforest Siberians: www.iceforestsiberians.com

* Lavalier Siberians: lavaliercats.com

* Murlyka Siberian Cattery: www.siberiankittens.ca

* Hairy Huddle: www.limpraha.cz/hh

* Wild Taiga: www.wildtaiga.unas.cz

* Lendal Siberians: lendal-sib.dk

* Nelius Siberians: nelius.dk/velkommen

* Meldgaards Siberians: www.katterimeldgaards-sibirisk.dk/velkommen

* Kestilinnan Siberians: www.kestilinnankissala.tarinoi.net

* Ag-Bars Siberians: www.aqbars.com

* Amurin Siberians: www.amurin.net

* Sibcoon Siberians: www.sibcoons.com

* Kissintassun Siberians: www.kissintassun.net

* Artannes' Cattery: chatsiberien.net/index_langEN_us.htm

* Abakan Forest: www.abakanforest.fr/index_en.html

* Chatterie des Dolgans: lesdolgans.jimdo.com

* Bajun Siberians: www.bajuns.de

* Spirit of New Heaven's Siberians: www.sibi-cats.de

* Forestwind Siberian Cats: www.sweetsiberians.com/siberiancatbreeders.htm

* Sineglazka Siberian Cats: www.sineglazkasiberiancats.com

* Skyblue Siberians: www.skyebluesiberians.com/about-us.html

* Musrafy Siberian Cats: musrafy.co.uk

* Silver Siberian Cats: www.silversiberiancats.co.uk

* Druzhina Siberian Cats: www.druzhina-siberian-cats.co.uk

Chapter 6. Basic Care of your Siberian Cat

So you have done your research, found a breeder and are now the proud owner of a Siberian Cat. Congratulations, that is wonderful and you are sure to have years of enjoyment with your cat.

However, bringing home a kitten isn't the end of things and it is important to bring your kitten home properly and to also make them feel comfortable when they come home.

In this chapter, I will go over bringing your kitten home, setting up routines and everything you need to know about handling and playing with your Siberian Cat.

1. Introducing your Kitten to Its Home

One of the most important steps to owning a Siberian Cat is introducing the cat into your home. If you do it properly, the cat will quickly relax into their new home and this will make life more enjoyable with your Siberian Cat.

a) Settling in the Home

When you first bring your kitten home, there will be a period of time for the kitten to adjust. This is the same for adult cats as well. Most kittens will take a few days to a week to relax enough and some cats can take up to a year before they feel comfortable and confident in their new home.

Don't be discouraged if the cat does not settle into your home immediately and simply keep providing the cat with stability, food and love and your kitten will adjust.

When you first bring your kitten or cat home, bring it into a room. Don't leave the kitten or cat to run free in the home, as you want him to become comfortable and familiar with the surroundings.

The best way to start this is to set up the litter box, food dishes and a bed in a room that can be closed off. In the bed, place a ticking clock and a water bottle so the kitten can snuggle into it for comfort.

Place the Siberian Cat into the room and close the door.

Give him a few hours to relax and then go in and sit with him for a little while. Repeat often throughout the day as your Siberian Cat becomes more comfortable with you and with his new home.

Although you may be eager to show your Siberian Cat the rest of his home, avoid doing this. Instead, let him stay in his room for the first 2 to 3 days. When he becomes comfortable with you and with his environment, open it up and gradually allow him access to the rest of the house. Repeat the process and allow him to explore instead of forcing it on him.

While the process may seem long, it will give your kitten the best start and you will find that your kitten is confident in his new home in no time.

b) Introducing Pets into the Home

Another step to getting your Siberian Cat used to his new home is by introducing him to other pets in the home. If you do not have any other pets, then this process can be skipped.

If you do, it is very important for you to remember that introducing pets takes time. When you bring a second cat into the home, it can take up to a year before they accept each other. A relationship between an older dog and a cat can also take a great deal of time. Not only does your kitten have to become comfortable with your current pet but the reverse has to occur as well.

The key to success is to separate your new cat when you bring him home. Make sure the room you are keeping him in is away from the other animals. In addition, don't even allow your other pets to sniff at the door for the first day or two. This can be quite stressing to both animals.

Before you go into the kitten's room, interact with your older pet and make sure you get his scent on you. After that, go in and allow the kitten to smell you. Before you leave, make sure that you rub him and get the scent of the kitten on you.

47

By doing this, both animals will get used to the smell of each other and it can make introductions easier.

After a day or so, allow the animals to sniff at each other from under the door. Don't comfort the animals when they show any distress at the new scent. The reason for this is that your comfort could send them the message that their distress is okay.

The next stage would be to open the door and allow the animals to interact. Watch them carefully and only step in if you see any sign that one will be injured. When you can't watch them, keep them segregated.

Always allow the animals to interact on their own terms. Don't force the interaction as this could cause more problems for both pets. Take things slowly as the animals will decide on their own to become friends – even though it may take a few months to a year for it to happen.

c) Introducing to Children

The final introduction that you should make is with any children that you have. Often, it can be difficult for children to be relaxed for the introduction, which can make a calm introduction difficult.

The best thing to do is to bring the kitten home and place him in his room. Let the kids know that the kitten needs to rest before an introduction. After a few hours, take the children into the room and have them sit down. Allow the kitten to come and explore them.

As they do, explain the rules about the kitten. Teach them how to handle the Siberian Cat and make sure that they learn to never bother the cat when they are sleeping or eating.

Keep the visits short and have periods where only one child goes in at a time. Make sure that they remain sitting so they don't startle the kitten or hurt it.

As the kitten's world opens up to your entire home, follow through on the rules of handling with your kids. Also, if your children are very young, never allow them to be alone with the kitten. It can be very easy for a toddler to hurt a kitten.

One thing that you should take with introduction is time. Do things gradually and without pushing the cat. If you do this, your Siberian Cat will quickly settle in to his new home.

2. Basic Routines and Care

When it comes to basic routines and care, there really isn't a lot that you need to do with a Siberian Cat. They are a pretty easy cat to own and aren't really demanding.

On a daily basis, you should take the time to spend it with your Siberian Cat. As I have mentioned about their personality, they are affectionate and love being with their owners. Not having that time with their owners can lead to them becoming withdrawn and depressed.

In addition to playing with your Siberian Cat, you should set up a routine for them. Trust me, if cats know that you feed them as soon as you wake up, they will quickly begin waking you up for their food.

Instead, make a routine for your feeding. Do a few different things when you wake up and feed your cat before you leave the house. The goal is to make a separation between feeding time and the other routines in your morning to prevent a frustrated kitten at your feet or waking you up.

Generally, in a daily routine, you should try to feed your Siberian Cat twice a day. The best routine is a morning and afternoon meal. Grooming is not something that is necessary every day but you should take 5 minutes to do a quick health check.

The other things that need to be done on a daily basis is playtime and cleaning out the litter box. Keeping a clean litter box will help with keeping the kitten going in the box. Some cats don't mind a box with some dirt in it, however, other cats will stop going immediately if the box is dirty.

3. Handling your Siberian Cat

The last thing that I want to touch on in this chapter is the overall handling of your Siberian Cat. This is important for building trust with your cat and will help with building a bond. Properly handling a cat will keep you both happy and the cat will enjoy the experience of being handled.

It is very important that you make it a daily task to touch and hold your cat. This will help condition your cat to touch and will make sure that he is accepting of being held and touched.

When you first start out, always make sure that your Siberian Cat is resting comfortably. Don't choose a time when your cat wants to play or is feeling stressed as that will only lead to the cat feeling overwhelmed and possibly lashing out.

Once your cat is settled, sit beside him but do not place him on your lap. If he wants to go onto your lap during the exercise, do so but if not, let him sit where he wants.

Next, begin petting him in a way that you know he enjoys. Always start with this positive treatment so he can relax further as the exercise goes on. Praise him while he remains calm.

After a few minutes, work your way down to areas that he may not like being touched. Run your hand down his back, down his tail and on his sides. Pet his feet and his belly. Work slowly and praise when he is relaxed. If he tenses up, remove your hand and allow him to settle again.

Give your Siberian Cat the odd treat as you are handling him so he views the treatment as a positive experience. Repeat on a daily basis and as he becomes more accustomed to being handled, begin handling sensitive areas. These areas include:

* Holding his ear to look into it.
* Lifting up his paws and examining the toes and claws.
* Opening up the lips and looking in the mouth.
* Touching his belly.
* Holding his tail firmly.

Remember to go patiently, praise and treat. If he becomes anxious, stop touching the sensitive areas and go back to petting an area that he enjoys. Do not treat him while he is anxious. By doing this, eventually your Siberian Cat will have no problem with being touched in any manner.

Chapter 7. Training your Siberian Cat

Although many people view training as something that you would do with a dog, you can train a Siberian Cat to do various tricks. Actually, you can teach your cat a wide variety of tricks so never feel limited by owning a cat.

The Siberian Cat, specifically, is very intelligent and will take to training quite easy. It is also beneficial to your Siberian Cat since they can get bored very easily and training helps keep them occupied.

1. Litter Training a Siberian Cat

While many people believe that the mama cat will litter train her kittens, this is actually a myth and is something that is taught by the breeder and also by the owner.

Never assume that a kitten is litter box trained when you first bring it home. This is the same for an adult Siberian Cat. Take the time to show the cat where the litter box is when you bring him home.

To do this, have a clean litter box ready in the location that you want it to be in. Place the kitten or cat into the box and rub his paws in the litter box. Keep calm and if the cat appears agitated, leave him alone but repeat the process later.

Once he is familiar with the litter box, keep an eye on him to be sure that he is defecating and urinating in the box. If you don't see him doing so, continually place him in the box whenever you think would be a good time.

Generally, kittens go to the bathroom after they wake up, after they drink and after they eat. Also, kittens will often have to go to the bathroom shortly after they have a play session.

After those times, pick up the kitten and place him in the kitty litter, again, move his paws into the clay so the kitten becomes interested in it.

As you are waiting for the kitten to go to the bathroom, keep it calm. Stroke you Siberian Cat and praise it while it is in the kitty litter. When your cat does eliminate, praise your kitten with a calm voice and pet him. Give him a treat when he is out of the litter box.

Immediately clean up the litter box. Remember, leaving it messy could lead to your kitten soiling the carpets and other areas of your home.

Be patient with litter box training. Your kitten will get it eventually.

2. Leash Training your Siberian Cat

Another area of training that you can do with your cat is leash training. This is not necessary for all cats but if you want to take your Siberian Cat outside for walks to enjoy the fresh air, the safest way to do so is if he is on a lead.

While many people don't think cats can learn to leash train, it is actually quite easy to teach a cat to accept it. Like anything else that you are training a cat to do, it is important to take leash training slowly and to do it gradually.

With leash training, I recommend that you purchase a good harness and a strong, 6 to 8-foot leash. Don't use a collar as this can hurt the delicate muscles in a cat's neck.

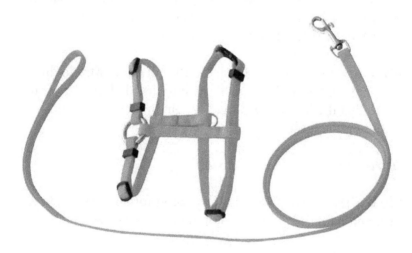

For successful leash training, follow these steps:

Step One: Introduce the Harness

The first step to training your Siberian Cat to walk on the leash is to condition him to the harness. This is done by simply placing the harness on the cat and leaving it on for short intervals.

Don't pull on the cat with the harness as all you want him to do is get used to the actual weight and feel of the harness. Instead, give him treats while he is in the harness and praise him while he is calm.

Do this for 20 to 30 minute periods throughout the day and practice with just the harness for two or three days until he is comfortable with the harness.

Step Two: Introduce the Leash

Once the Siberian Cat is comfortable with the harness, it is time to start introducing the leash. This is a tricky stage, as you want to keep the kitten safe without scaring him. I recommend that you get a shorter leash for this stage but it is not necessary. The shorter leash is just less likely to get tangled.

When you first introduce the leash, don't pull on it or try to direct the cat in any direction. Instead, allow it to drag behind the cat to make sure that the leash doesn't get caught up in anything but avoid holding the leash at any other time.

Step Three: Introduce some Tension

Only do this step if your Siberian Cat is comfortable with having the leash and harness on. If he is not, don't move on with this step.

If your cat is comfortable with the leash and harness, you can begin the next stage of leash training, which is adding some tension to the leash.

Pick up the leash and walk with your cat in the direction that he is walking. Don't try to get him to go where you want him by pulling on the lead. Instead, offer him a treat to get him to move forward or in the direction you want to take him.

If he doesn't move at all, pick him up and move him about a foot in the direction you want. Treat and praise him for moving and encourage him to move again.

Repeat this process for 8 to 10 minutes and then take a break for an hour or two and repeat again. Do it 4 to 8 times in a day as your schedule allows.

Step Number Four: Apply Direction

Now that your cat is used to you using the leash, apply some tension to get the cat to move in the direction that you want. In the beginning, make sure that you use some treats as well as tension. Praise the cat when he is doing a great job and give him plenty of treats.

Step Number Five: Make the Harness Fun

The final step that you want to do is to trick your Siberian Cat into thinking that the harness is a fun thing. The best way to do this is to do the exercises with the cat and give him plenty of praise and treats.

After the 8 or 10 minutes, take the harness off of the Siberian Cat. Then ignore the cat for an hour or two. Don't pet him or give him any treats and don't feed him during this period.

After the allotted time, go back, place the harness and leash on him and then give him attention, praise and treats. The cat will quickly learn that the harness is a good thing.

When he begins to accept the harness, you can begin giving him attention both when he is on the harness and off.

It can take a few days or weeks to get a kitten used to walking on the lead, but once you do, your Siberian Cat will be happy and eager to go for a walk.

3. Tricks for your Siberian Cat

While there are a number of different tricks that you can train your cat to do, I am only going to go over a few of those tricks. The main reason for this is that once you learn how to train one command, you can train your cat to learn any command.

There are three important tips with training that you will use with all training methods with your cat. These are:

Tip Number One: Use Food

Believe it or not, cats are as food driven as dogs can be and they will learn when they get treats. In addition, you can use treats for baiting the cat to do what you would like him to do. Hold the treat out and simply guide him with the treat into the trick.

Tip Number Two: Be Patient

Always be patient when you are training a cat. In general, Siberian Cats have their own minds and they may take a bit of time to get into a trick. The main reason for this is because cats don't feel the need to please you, they need to be in the mood to want to please you.

What this means is that a trick may take more time. Also, training sessions are usually more informal and are done when the cat has decided and not the trainer. It also means that your cat may have sessions when he completely ignores you.

When this happens, don't get frustrated and don't give him. Instead, ignore the cat and make sure you don't give him any praise, attention or treats until he is willing to work with you.

Tip Number Three: Work Gradually

Finally, make sure you work on a trick gradually. It may take weeks for you to teach your Siberian Cat to shake a paw and that is okay. Always work within your cat's comfort zone, if he becomes agitated stop and then go back to the command later.

In addition, only work on one command at a time. Wait until he has mastered the one command before you start on a new command.

a) Come

Come is actually a very easy command to teach your cat and it is one of the commands that you can teach without doing any planned training sessions.

Instead, train come at meal times and follow these steps.

1. To start, take the food bowl into your hands.

2. Say your cat's name and immediately say, "Come."

3. Tap the food bowl and place food into it.

4. When he/she comes to the sound of the food, praise your cat and pet him.

5. Set the food down as the reward.

6. Repeat at every mealtime.

b) Sit Up/Dance

With sit up or dance, you want to decide which command you want to teach your cat. If you simply want him/her to sit up, the cat would remain on its haunches but if you want it to dance, you will need for him/her to stand slightly on the back legs.

This is another easy trick to teach your cat and it uses the same technique regardless of whether you are teaching sit up or dance.

1. Place a cat treat in your hand and show it to your Siberian Cat.

2. Raise the treat over your cat's head. You should place it slightly above his head for sit up and up higher for dance.

3. Give the command, "Sit up."

3. Your cat should follow the treat and will sit up to grab at the treat with its paws. Allow this to happen and praise him for sitting up.

4. If you are teaching dance, you can slowly work the training so that your cat turns when he is standing up.

5. Praise the cat when he is on his haunches and treat immediately.

c) Shake a Paw

Shake a paw is a command that you should only teach after your cat is accustomed to having its feet touched. If he doesn't like it, avoid doing this command.

1. Have your cat sit in front of you.

2. Give the command, "Shake," and touch his paw.

3. If he doesn't lift his paw when you touch it, pick up the paw yourself. If he does lift it, take the paw into your hand and shake gently.

4. Praise the cat as you are shaking the paw and then give a treat.

5. Repeat 10 to 15 times in a row as your Siberian Cat allows.

d) Wave

The final trick that I am going to go over is teaching your Siberian Cat to wave. This actually uses a natural habit of most cats and makes it into a cute trick.

1. Have the cat sit in front of you.

2. Take a treat and place it in your hand.

3. Hold the treat right in front of the cat's nose and then move it back slightly so the treat is out of reach for the cat.

4. Wait until the cat tries to paw at the treat and then give the command, "Wave."

5. Move the treat back and forth in a waving motion to encourage the cat to wave.

6. Praise and treat the cat.

And there are some tricks that you can train your cat to do.

Chapter 8. Grooming your Siberian Cat

As you know, the Siberian Cat has a moderately long coat that will require some grooming. While other breeds with long coats require quite a bit of grooming time, the Siberian Cat is not one of those.

In fact, the Siberian Cat is fairly easy to groom and outside of basic maintenance, there really isn't a lot that you need to do to keep the coat looking its best. One thing that should be pointed out is whether you are showing your cat or not. If you are, you will need to groom your cat more frequently than you would for a companion pet.

In this chapter, I will go over everything you need to know about grooming your Siberian Cat.

Before I do, however, I want to stress the importance of grooming your cat at a young age. Cats can become very accustomed to grooming and grooming becomes very easy when you start them young.

In addition, taking the time to groom your Siberian Cat can help you in maintaining the health of your pet. Whenever you groom your cat, take the time to check over his skin to make sure it is free from fleas.

1. Brushing your Siberian Cat

The very first thing that we should look at with grooming is brushing your Siberian Cat. On average, you should try to brush your cat's coat about once per week. Less than that and your cat's coat may tangle and become matted.

One thing that should be mentioned is that Siberian Cats have a coat that does not mat easily. It is actually quite low maintenance, however, during times of the year when there is shedding, you should make sure that you brush the coat on a daily basis.

That being said, let's go over the steps to brushing your cat. Before we do, it is important to have the proper tools for your cat's coat type. Longhaired breeds should use the following brushes:

* *Slicker:* Choose a good quality slicker brush for your cat. This will often be the main brush that you use for your Siberian Cat.

* *Undercoat Brush*: The Siberian Cat does have an undercoat and will require an undercoat brush, especially during shedding season.

* *Flea Comb:* The final brush that you should have is a flea comb. These combs are used to brush the shorter hair of your Siberian Cat.

And that is all you really need to brush your Siberian Cat out and keep him looking his best. To brush a cat, follow these steps:

1. Find a relaxing area for your cat to be brushed out on. It is better if the cat is relaxed and calm so try to do it in an area where he can lay down and enjoy his grooming time.

2. Start at one area of the cat; work in small sections and not across the entire cat.

3. Taking the slicker brush, brush in the opposite direction of the hair growth to remove dead and loose hair.

4. Once it is brushed out, take the undercoat brush and begin brushing in the direction of the hair growth. When you are

brushing, remove the hair often or you can create new mats in the coat.

5. Once the entire cat is brushed, run the slicker brush through the coat once more to smooth out the hair.

6. Take the flea comb and brush the hair on the face and head and also on the legs.

7. When you are done, wipe the cat down with a chamois cloth. The reason for this is that it will leave the Siberian Cat looking silky and will create a nice sheen on the coat. It will also remove any dead hair that you missed.

If you find that the coat has a lot of mats to it, you can take a de-matting comb and carefully pick the mat out of the coat. Be sure to work until the cat starts to struggle and then stop.

Brushing your Siberian Cat does not have to be difficult and since this is a cat that doesn't suffer from a lot of coat problems, you can usually limit the amount of grooming you do in a week.

2. Bathing your Siberian Cat

Another part of grooming that doesn't need to be done frequently is bathing. Cats are naturally clean animals and the Siberian Cat is no different. Still, you should make the effort to bathe your Siberian Cat every few weeks to keep the amount of dander to a minimum.

With bathing, it is best to start getting your cat familiar with water at a young age. Frequent baths when your Siberian Cat is a kitten will help with him accepting, and even enjoying, his baths as an adult. When he gets older, you can start to limit the number of baths.

During bath time, it is always important to keep it very calm and relaxing to the cat. For that reason, it is better to choose a bathing time when the cat is at his most relaxed.

Although you can use any type of pet shampoo for your Siberian Cat, I recommend using a shampoo that is designed for long haired felines. To bathe your cat, follow the steps below.

1. Brush your cat before you give the cat a bath.

2. Clip the claws of your Siberian Cat before you give him a bath.

3. Place the cat in a sink or a tub.

4. Fill the tub with 3 to 4 inches of warm water. If the cat is scared of running water, fill the sink prior to washing.

5. With a pitcher, pour water over the cat's coat. Avoid getting it directly onto the face and in the ears as this can cause problems for your cat.

6. Once the coat is wet, lather on the cat shampoo. Start on the head and carefully work down the body of the cat. Make sure you avoid the face to prevent soap getting in the eyes and ears.

7. Once the cat has been lathered up, rinse the shampoo off with a pitcher or a spray hose if your cat will tolerate it. You may have to add new water to the sink. Wash thoroughly as soap that is left in the fur can lead to irritation on the skin.

8. Wring the fur of the cat to remove as much water as possible.

9. Take a washcloth and carefully wipe the Siberian Cat's face to remove any dirt. Do not use soap unless the face is very dirty. In that case, use diluted soap and carefully wash and rinse with the washcloth.

10. Wrap the cat in a towel and towel dry the cat. If your Siberian Cat will allow, dry the coat with a blow dryer on the lowest setting.

11. When the cat is dry, brush out the coat to keep it from matting or tangling.

Bathing a cat can be difficult if you have not accustomed it to water so be prepared for a fight. Thankfully, Siberian Cats generally love water so they often don't fight at bath time.

3. Clipping your Siberian Cat's Nails

Nail clipping is an important part of caring for your Siberian Cat and it will help prevent some frustration for you. A cat who undergoes frequent nail trimming will be less likely to sharpen his claws on your furniture. In addition, keeping the nails clipped short will help minimize damage if the cat swats at you.

Before you trim your cat's nails, make sure that you have the right supplies. You will need:

* Cat Nail Trimmers

* Emery Board

* Styptic Powder

When you are trimming your cat's nails, it is important to make your cat relax before you begin. To do this, sit with him in your lap facing out. This is the best position when you start clipping the nails so it is good to start this way.

Pet the cat until he relaxes his body and then touch his feet. Start handling the feet through the petting session but watch his cues.

If he becomes agitated, simply put the paw down and continue massaging your Siberian Cat.

When he is finally relaxed, you can begin clipping the nails. To clip the nails, do the following:

1. Grab the paw that will be clipped and press on the knuckle to make the nail extend. You do not have to push hard for this to occur.

2. Inspect the nail and nail bed. Check for any cracks or injury near the nail bed and on the nail. Also look for the quick, which is the vein running through the center of the claw.

3. Place the cat nail trimmers at a 90° angle onto the nail. Line it up to the quick so you are cutting the nail right before the quick. If you can't see the quick, take off just a small amount of nail to prevent cutting the quick.

4. Make a clean cut of the nail, removing the sharp bit of nail.

5. Repeat on all of the nails on the paw and also do the dewclaw.

6. Take the emery board and sand down any rough or sharp edges on the cut claw.

7. Repeat on the other paws.

8. If you cut the quick when you are clipping the claws, dip the claw in the styptic powder immediately. This will stop the bleeding.

Although you can clip the back claws, many people find that they do not need to clip the back claws as often as they clip the front claws. Only clip a claw if it is necessary so you don't cut the quick.

4. Ear Cleaning

As I have said several times through this book, cats don't require a lot of grooming since they are naturally clean animals. However, there will be the occasional when you need to clean your Siberian Cat's ears, especially if the cat has ear mites or an infection in the ear.

To clean a cat's ears, you will need:

* Cotton Balls
* Ear Cleaning Solution
* Tweezers
* Eyebrow Scissors

Cleaning the ears is very simple and shouldn't take any time. You should do it when your Siberian Cat is relaxed to help reduce the amount of stress that he feels.

1. Check the inside of the ear and remove any large debris from the ear with tweezers.

2. Using eyebrow scissors, carefully trim any long hair that is irritating the ear canal or blocking it. Make sure you remove the hair that you have trimmed.

3. Soak a cotton ball with ear cleaning solution.

4. Place the cotton ball into the ear but do not press it down into the ear canal.

5. Massage the area around the cotton ball so the cotton ball will pick up the dirt.

6. Remove the cotton ball, wiping away any excess dirt or solution.

7. Repeat in the other ear.

And that is all there is to cleaning the ear. It is very simple and should only take a few minutes at most.

5. Teeth Brushing

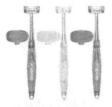

The final area of grooming that we are going to cover is teeth brushing. This is very important with Siberian Cats, as they can be prone to gum disease.

To brush a Siberian Cat's teeth, you should have:

* Cat Toothbrush

* Cat Toothpaste; do not use human toothpaste

Cats can be difficult patients when it comes to teeth cleaning so it is very important that you get your Siberian Cat used to having things in his mouth at a young age. Start with your fingers and then move up to cotton swabs and finally to a toothbrush designed for cats. This should take several sessions before your cat will accept a toothbrush.

1. Place a pea sized amount of toothpaste on the toothbrush.

2. Pull up the cat's lips.

3. In gentle movements, run the toothbrush over the cat's teeth and gums. Be sure to get the gums as this will help prevent gum disease.

4. Start at the top of the mouth and brush all the top teeth before moving to the bottom teeth.

When you are done, praise the kitten and give him a dental treat. In between brushing, you can offer dental treats to prevent a build up of plague.

Chapter 9. Feeding your Siberian Cat

For many people, feeding their cat is as simple as pouring out a bowl of dry cat food and letting the cat moderate its own intake. However, it shouldn't be that easy because feeding a cat in this manner can lead to many different health problems.

The main reason for this is that many cat foods do not have the proper nutrition for cats. The second is that we often get roped into the latest trend – among those being the vegetarian diet for cats. And the third is that cats need a range of foods for a complete diet.

For that reason, more should be put into deciding on the food and how to feed your cat than simply filling a bowl with food. In this chapter, I will go over everything that you need to know about feeding your Siberian Cat.

1. Nutrition for your Siberian Cat

One of the most widely debated topics regarding cats in general is often the food. Many people disagree with the latest fads or they wonder exactly what is an important part of their cat's nutrition.

Thankfully, it doesn't have to be difficult to figure out and it comes down to simple facts about the important nutrients that your pet needs. While many cat foods say they are complete, it is important to read the ingredients and make sure that they have the following nutrients:

Protein

If there is a nutrient that is an absolute must for your Siberian Cat, it is protein. Cats require food that is strictly made of animal based proteins. The reason for this is because cats are carnivores and while they may add some vegetables to their diet without too many problems, eating a strictly vegetarian meal will cause several disorders in your Siberian Cat.

Proteins are filled with amino acids, which are important nutrients for tissue growth. In fact, they are called the body's "building blocks" and cats can manufacture 12 of the 23 amino acids used for tissue growth. The rest comes from dietary means through animal proteins or vegetable proteins.

While there are proteins in vegetables, they generally have a lower biological value than meat proteins, especially for cats. In addition, the amino acid known as taurine is only found in animal tissues.

Taurine is considered to be one of the most important amino acids for cats since it helps them sustain their cardiovascular, visual and reproductive performance. A diet that is missing animal proteins will decrease a cat's quality of life.

Another important amino acid that is found in meat is arginine. This amino acid promotes detoxification and helps in removing nitrogenous waste from the cat's body.

If a cat does not receive the proper nutrients, the body will stop functioning properly.

Fat

Another important nutrient for cats to get in their diet is fat. Fat is important because it works in several ways:

1. It supplies energy to the Siberian Cat.

2. It helps absorb fat-soluble vitamins such as vitamins A, D, E and K.

3. It provides essential fatty acids, which promote better health and function.

4. It makes food taste better to cats.

5. It promotes healthy skin and coats.

As you can see, there are many different benefits to having a food that is rich in fats. Another big benefit is that fat offers a cat both linoleic acid and arachidonic acid, which help the cat's body function on a day to day basis.

However, there is a side effect to too much fat and that is simply that the cat can become obese, so be sure to find a well balanced food.

Carbohydrates

One problem that has been seen frequently in commercial cat food is that there is an abundance of carbohydrates in a cat's diet. While some carbohydrates are healthy and will actually provide a Siberian cat with energy, many carbohydrates are broken down into starches and sugars, which lead to obesity in your cat.

For foods, it is important to choose a commercial cat food that is only 35% carbohydrates. This lower amount is very easy for cats to live with, especially since carbohydrates are grain and vegetable derived. Any more of a percentage in the food and your Siberian Cat will quickly become obese.

Vitamins and Minerals

When you are deciding on a cat food, make sure that you take the time to go over the vitamins and minerals that the food has. Make sure you find one that is listed as a complete or balanced food. These terms in the description of the food mean that they have the proper balance of vitamins and minerals to keep your Siberian Cat healthy.

With Siberian Cats, you want to look at the following vitamins and minerals in their diet:

* *Vitamin A:* This is an important vitamin but you want to find a food that has preformed vitamin A. Many foods use beta-carotene and cats cannot convert beta-carotene into vitamin A like other animals so avoid foods that list beta-carotene as the only source of vitamin A.

* *Vitamin B:* This includes thiamine and niacin, but cats usually require more vitamin B than other animals.

* *Calcium:* Calcium is important because it helps with the bones and teeth of the cat, as well as other bodily functions.

* *Vitamin D:* While you can get vitamin D from sunlight, cats, especially Siberian Cats that live inside, will need it in their cat food.

* *Vitamin E:* Vitamin E is important for the body to function properly, it can only be absorbed by fat, which is why fat is important in a cat's diet.

* *Vitamin K:* Vitamin K is another important vitamin and like vitamin E, it needs fat to be absorbed by the Siberian Cat's body.

* *Phosphorous:* Finally, for the same reason as calcium, you should make sure that your Siberian Cat's food offers phosphorous.

One vitamin that you want to avoid with cats is vitamin C since cats make the vitamin on their own.

In addition, you should never supplement a cat with vitamins and minerals; instead, use a complete or balanced food. Supplements can lead to over supplementation, which can cause serious diseases and even death in your Siberian Cat.

Water

While water is not something that is in the food you give your cat, it is an important part of nutrition for cats. Unlike many animals, cats have a high need for water. In fact, cats have a stronger thirst drive than other mammals and need constant access to fresh water.

In addition, it is important to offer a combination of wet and dry food so your Siberian Cat will get water in his food. Wet cat food is made of 75% water and this can help boost the amount of water your cat gets in a day.

2. Choosing the Right Food

Now that you know what nutrients your Siberian Cat needs, it is time to look at how to choose the right food for your Siberian

Cat. While it may seem like a big task, once you get used to looking at the label and understanding food, choosing the right food is simple – all you need to do is follow these tips:

Tip Number One: Look at the Label

The very first thing that you should do is look at the label. You are actually looking for a few different things but specifically, you want to make sure of a few things:

1. That is says AAFCO. Make sure the food has been approved by the AAFCO. If it hasn't, choose a different food.

2. Make sure it says balanced or complete. This means that a feline nutritionist has gone over the ingredients and feels that it has everything a cat needs.

3. Has a valid expiration date. Yes, cat food can go bad so always check the expiration date. No expiration date? Don't buy it.

Tip Number Two: Meat should be Present

When you are looking at the label, always check the ingredients list. You want to make sure that the meat that is in the food is a named meat such as chicken or lamb. Never use a food that simply lists it as meat. What this means is that it can be any type of meat used, which can have no nutritional value.

In addition to having the meats named, they should be the first three ingredients on the ingredients list. If they aren't, choose a different cat food.

Tip Number Three: Use Wet and Dry

There is some debate on whether you should use wet or dry cat food for your kitten and cat. The answer is simple; use both. The reason why I recommend this is because dry cat food is an excellent food to leave out for your cat to free feed on. In addition, the dry food will help clean the teeth and provides them with many of the nutrients that they need.

Wet cat food offers them a higher protein level, which they need, as well as more water. Feeding them a good quality, wet cat food will keep them healthy and feeling full for longer.

Also, cats tend to get bored of their food very easily so it is important to switch up the food on a regular basis. This will keep your Siberian Cat happy and will keep him eating.

Tip Number Four: Avoid Certain Ingredients

While you are reading those ingredient lists, you want to look for certain foods to avoid. These are:

* *By-products:* By-products usually mean that they are only adding the bad part of something. For instant, chicken by-products are usually things like the beaks and feet.

* *Meals:* Like by-products, meals are mainly made with low quality ingredients.

* *Chemicals:* Avoid foods that have a lot of preservatives such as ethoxyquin and BHA.

* *Corn:* A lot of cat food manufacturers will add corn into their foods. This gives your cat no nutritional value and manufacturers only use it as a filler.

* *Sugar:* Cats don't need sugars so avoid foods that have a lot of sugars in the ingredient lists.

Tip Number Five: Feed to Life Stages

Believe it or not, feeding to life stages is very important for your Siberian Cat. As the cat ages, it requires different levels of nutrients and the foods are specially formulated for that reason. Kittens should eat kitten food and senior cats should eat senior food. Don't choose a whole life food to avoid the extra cost. Trust me; a few extra dollars will be worth it in the long run.

And that is all you need to know about choosing the right food for your Siberian Cat.

3. Feeding your Siberian Cat

The final point that I want to go over in this chapter is when to feed your cat and how much you should feed him. As you may be aware of, the age of your cat will affect how you feed him. It is important to read the labels on your cat food and follow the recommendations on the label.

Regardless of the amount of food that you feed your cat, you should try to feed them more than once a day. Many cats will do very well eating once per day, however, it is not ideal.

Instead, feed the cat in the morning, preferably with a wet cat food. When the cat is finished, fill a bowl with dry kibble for the cat to eat through the day.

If you prefer not to free feed your cat, you should feed him twice per day. You can mix in the dry kibble with the wet cat food or feed wet in the morning and dry in the evening.

Regardless of how you feed your cat, make sure that you give your Siberian Cat about 1 to 2 hours to eat before you pick up the dish. Cats are not like dogs and eat as soon as the food goes down. They often eat in small amounts and come back to it over the course of a few hours.

The main points with feeding are to choose a high quality food that has low carbohydrates and is a good source of animal proteins. After that, everything else will be easy with feeding your cat.

Chapter 10. Your Siberian Cat's Health

Now that you have an understanding of raising your Siberian Cat so he remains happy, it is time to look at how to keep your Siberian Cat healthy.

One thing that I should mention is that Siberian Cats are known to be quite hardy. There is not a high risk of illness and the number of illnesses that can affect the breed is quite low. With that being said, it is still important to follow the proper steps to ensure your Siberian Cat stays healthy throughout its life.

In this chapter, I will go over the various illnesses that can affect the Siberian Cat breed and also go over signs to determine if your cat is not well. Finally, I will touch briefly upon vaccinating your cat and yearly vet care that should be carried out, including when to spay or neuter your feline friend.

1. Signs of Illness

The very first thing that we should cover is how to tell if your Siberian Cat is unwell. Although many illnesses have distinct indicators that will alert the owner to an illness, there are some illnesses that do not. In these cases, it is important to monitor your Siberian Cat to make sure there is no hidden illness occurring.

Every day, you should take the time to check your cat over. Look for any rashes, cuts or fur loss that could indicate a problem. In addition, check the litter box to make sure there are no signs of loose bowel movements.

In addition to those signs, look for the following signs in your cat that indicate that there may be an illness present:

81

1. Vomiting:

It is important to distinguish between vomiting and hairballs. Coughing up a hairball, which should be fairly dry and consist of mostly hair, is very normal for cats, especially those with longer coats.

Vomiting will contain stomach fluids and partially digested foods. If your cat is vomiting, there is a very good chance that some illness is affecting it. Seek veterinary care if you see your cat vomiting.

2. Abnormal Bowel Movements:

I have already mentioned this but you should pay close attention to your Siberian Cat's bowel movements. If you see diarrheal in the litter box, it is important to monitor your cat. It could be something that your cat has eaten, however, if it persists for more than 2 days, seek medical help.

In addition, if the cat is not having bowel movements, it can be an indicator that something is wrong.

Finally, if you see any blood in your Siberian Cat's faeces, seek immediate medical attention.

3. Decreased Activity:

While Siberian Cats can be lazy from time to time, it is important to watch the activity level of your cat. Cats will have normal periods of alertness and play and a sign of illness can be a decrease in activity. If you find that your Siberian Cat does not have his usual activity level, monitor him. If he shows any other symptoms or his activity level decreases even more, seek the help of a veterinarian.

4. Changes in Urine:

This one is often harder to see and is more commonly seen if you clean the kitty litter on a daily basis. In general, if you notice a change in the urine, such as a change in colour, an increase or decrease in urinating or a change in smell, you can suspect an underlying illness.

In addition, if there is blood in the urine, it can be linked to bladder stones, which can be very serious, especially for male cats.

5. Decrease in Appetite:

Although every animal goes through periods when they don't seem to be eating, it is very important that you keep track of what your cat is eating. If there is a decrease in appetite, don't allow it to go on for more than two days before you seek the help of your veterinarian.

The main reason for this is because cats are severely affected by lack of food. When they do not eat, they can develop a fatty liver and this can be fatal to cats. If your Siberian Cat has stopped eating all together, seek the advice of your vet.

6. Coughing or Sneezing:

Another common sign that your cat may be sick is frequent coughing and sneezing. Remember that cats will cough and sneeze occasionally, just like people, with nothing being wrong. However, if there seems to be respiratory distress or your Siberian Cat is sneezing and coughing frequently, it may indicate a medical problem.

7. Stiffness

Any type of stiffness in the joints and limbs of your Siberian Cat can be a large indication that your cat is unwell. This can be anything from not being able to stand up to a stiff gait when walking.

8. Loss of Coordination

Cats are agile and nubile creatures and the Siberian Cat is no different. When there is a loss of coordination or agility, you can suspect an illness, and it is important to seek the advice of your veterinarian.

9. Hair Loss

I have already mentioned this but hair loss can be a very good indicator that there are underlying medical problems. Hair loss can be caused by stress as well, which is important to deal with in your cat.

10. Skin Rashes

Finally, if you see any skin rashes or any damage to the skin, you should monitor it to determine if there is an underlying medical condition. If it doesn't go away, it is important to seek the advice of your vet.

As you can see, there are many different signs that your Siberian Cat is ill, but many illnesses can be caught before they worsen.

2. How to Examine your Siberian Cat

One thing that I always recommend to people is that they take the time to do monthly examinations of their cats to ensure that they are healthy. These are fairly easy to do and if you start at a young age, your Siberian Cat will come to enjoy these examinations.

In addition, these examinations will give you the reassurance that your Siberian Cat is healthy and will allow you to catch any illnesses when they first occur.

While you should always keep an eye on the health of your cat with an exam, you will need to do a bit more than simply watch for signs of illness. Instead, you should place your cat on a table or a safe location with good lighting and check over your entire cat.

When you do an exam, you will want to check the following:

Eyes:

Look into your cat's eyes and check the area around the eyes as well as the eye itself. Look for signs that there may be a problem such as:

- Weeping or tearstains
- Redness in the eye and around the eye
- Swelling around the eye
- Unusual Discharge
- Cloudy and dull

Nose:

After you look in the eyes, check the nose. A healthy Siberian Cat should have a nose that is moist or slightly dry, however, if you find that there is a lot of mucal discharge or the nose is starting to crack, it may indicate a problem. Other things to look for are:

- Bumps
- Sores
- Bleeding from the nostrils

- Swelling
- Unusual bumps

Chin:

Another area to check is the chin of your feline and make sure that there are no bumps on the skin. If the chin is dirty, take the time to wipe it clean to prevent problems such as acne.

Ears:

Ears that are dirty and seem to have a lot of wax often indicate a problem for the cat. In general, a Siberian cat should have clean, dry ears that do not have any odour to them, or any unpleasant odours.

When you are checking the ears, look for the following signs of infection or illness:

- Scratch marks
- Bleeding
- Scaling in the ear
- Redness
- Sores or lesions
- discharge in the ear that resembles ground coffee
- Lumps
- Swelling
- Thickening of the ear

Mouth:

I always recommend that you start your exam on the head of the cat so it is important to take the time to look at and in your Siberian Cat's mouth. When you check the mouth, make sure that you also check the teeth and gums. Look for the following symptoms that an illness is present:

1. Teeth

- Missing Teeth
- Sores on the gum line near the tooth
- Chips in the teeth
- Discolouration of the teeth

2. Gums

- Redness
- Pale gums
- Swelling in the gums
- Sores or lesions
- Bleeding

3. Mouth

- Swelling of the lips or on the tongue
- Lesions
- Lumps
- Ulcers on the lips or tongue

Be sure to check around the outside of the mouth as well as inside.

Claws:

When you are examining your cat, make sure that you take a look at the claws. Make sure that they are a healthy length but if they are too long, trim them. In addition, look for the following:

- Broken claws
- Missing claws
- Bleeding on the toe
- Swelling near the claw

Skin and Coat:

I always recommend that you look at the coat and skin at the same time. In addition, make sure that you run your hands over the cat as you work so you can see the skin through the coat.

When you do an exam of the skin and coat, check for the following:

- Dull fur
- Hair loss
- Dander in the fur
- Bugs such as fleas or mites
- Rashes
- Lesions
- Scratch marks or wounds

When you are checking the skin, make sure that you gently pull up on the skin. This should be done on the shoulder area. When you release, watch how quickly it falls back against the skin. If it springs back immediately, the cat is healthy; however, if it takes a long time to go back, it could indicate that your cat is dehydrated.

Respiration:

As you are working on the exam, check your cat's respiration. Make sure that the breathing is easy and deep. If the cat seems to be struggling to take a breath, this can be seen by panting, coughing or wheezing, then there may be an underlying medical problem.

Body:

Run your hands down your cat's body and check to make sure that he has a good weight on him. You should be able to feel the ribs just under a layer of flesh. If you can't feel the ribs, then your

Siberian Cat should be on a diet, if you can easily, your cat should get extra food or checked for an underlying problem.

In addition to checking your cat's weight, make sure that you feel the body to ensure that there are no lumps or unusual bumps. Make sure that you check the entire body including the legs and tail.

Mobility:

When you are done with the exam, put your cat down and then watch his movement for about 5 minutes. If he seems stiff or there is a loss of coordination, then there may be a health problem.

An exam shouldn't take more than 10 minutes and it can be a wonderful time to bond with your cat. If you see anything unusual, be sure to contact your veterinarian.

3.Spaying and Neutering your Siberian Cat

If you are planning on breeding your Siberian Cat, then you are not going to need to read this section of the book. Before you do choose to breed, however, it is important to stress that the cat population is extremely high. If you are breeding, make sure that you breed correctly to prevent your kittens from winding up in a shelter.

With that said, spaying and neutering is a very important step in cat ownership. Cats that are not used in a cattery should be spayed or neutered. Without spaying, your kitten can begin to have kittens of her own before the age of 6 months. Male cats will begin to spay at the age of 10 months, or younger.

Although I strongly recommend you discuss spaying and neutering with your veterinarian, to help you understand the process better, I am going to answer a few questions on spaying and neutering.

When to Spay and Neuter?

One question that many people are confused with is when to spay or neuter their cats. Veterinarians will often recommend any time after your cat is 4 months old, however, males that are neutered at a young age rarely develop the large heads of tomcats.

It is important to be aware of this, however, you should have your male Siberian Cat neutered between the ages of 4 and 10 months of age.

Female Siberian Cats can be spayed as young as 4 months old, however, it is recommended that you wait until your kitten is 6 months of age.

What is spaying?

Spaying is a surgery where the ovaries and uterus of a female animal is removed. Spaying only refers to the surgery done to

female animals and it can also be known as an
ovariohysterectomy. After the surgery, the cat should not be able
to reproduce and will not enter into heat cycles. See the chapter
on breeding to understand cat heats.

What is neutering?

Neutering refers to the surgery where the testicles of the cat are
removed. Neutering is only done to male animals. It is also
known as castration and prevents the cat from reproducing. It also
prevents much behaviour such as marking.

Does spaying and neutering hurt my Siberian Cat?

The short answer is that yes, spaying and neutering is painful
since it is a surgery. However, veterinarians will only perform the
procedures while the animal is under general anaesthesia.

In addition, the veterinarian will give specific instructions for
care after the surgery to ensure minimal discomfort for your pet.

In the long term, however, spaying and neutering does not cause
lifelong pain for your cat. In fact, most cats usually bounce back
from the surgery after a day or two and the surgery wound will be
completely healed within two weeks.

Are there any risks involved with spaying or neutering?

There are always risks involved during surgery, especially under
a general anaesthesia. However, spaying and neutering are
routine surgeries and the risks are minimal.

Will my Siberian Cat's personality change?

In general, you shouldn't notice any personality changes. If your
Siberian Cat is affectionate and friendly, you will find that he is
still affectionate and friendly after the surgery. That being said,

spaying and neutering often correct negative behaviours such as marking in the house.

In addition, many cats will appear to be more docile than before they were altered and they may be lazier than before their surgery. Things that don't seem to change are their overall personality, hunting skills and playfulness.

Spaying and neutering your cat is something that is strongly recommended to help control the pet population.

4. Vaccinations for your Siberian Cat

Although there is some debate on the frequency of vaccinations for your cat, many people agree that vaccinations are important for maintaining the health of your feline friend.

Vaccinations are injections that help boost the immune system of the patient receiving the vaccine. This boost enables the body to build up antibodies against specific diseases, which creates immunity to the disease.

Although many veterinarians will recommend a host of vaccinations on a yearly basis, more research has been done on the validity of this claim. In many cases, cats do not need to be vaccinated on a yearly basis and can go two or three years between vaccinations. If your Siberian Cat is an outdoor cat, however, you should consider giving your cat yearly vaccinations.

There are a range of vaccinations that you can get your cat, however, you should look at obtaining the core vaccinations at the very least for your cat.

a) Core Vaccinations

Core vaccinations are vaccinations that you should get for your Siberian Cat, especially when he is a kitten. Again, the frequency will differ depending on the risk to your cat. Cats that reside strictly indoors should only need the vaccination every 3 years, while cats that go outside should have them yearly.

FHV-1/FCV/FPV

While this vaccine has only one name it is actually a combination of vaccines that are given as one shot. The vaccines that you get in this shot are:

- *Feline Calicivirus (FCV):* This vaccine protects against a respiratory infection that is common in cats. It is administered several times when the cat is a kitten and then yearly for outdoor cats and every 3 years for indoor cats.

- *Feline Viral Rhinotracheitis (FVR):* Another vaccine that protects against a respiratory infection in cats. It is actually the vaccine used for the illness known as feline influenza. The disease itself is very serious and can lead to death in young kittens.

- *Feline Panleukopenia Virus (FPV):* The vaccine protects your cat against feline parvovirus, which is similar to canine parvovirus. It is commonly known as feline distemper and it can be fatal to your cat if he contracts the disease.

Rabies

The other core vaccine that is administered to kittens and cats is the rabies vaccine. This vaccine is actually disputed and many owners have been pushing to have the vaccine taken off as a core vaccine.

However, if rabies is prevalent in your area, it is considered to be a core vaccine since there is an increased risk of an animal contracting the illness. Without the rabies vaccine, the disease is fatal.

b) Non Core Vaccines

While there are core vaccines that should be given, there are also noncore vaccines that offer added protection to your Siberian Cat. It is important to note that noncore vaccines are not necessary and are only given to cats if there is a risk of the disease in the area.

- *Chlamydophila Felis:* This is an infection that can be very common in households that have multiple cats.

- *Feline Immunodeficiency Virus (FIV):* This is a serious infection that is similar to AIDS and is often referred to as Feline AIDS. The virus is very serious and can be fatal if it is contracted, which is why vets recommend the vaccine.

- *Feline Leukemia Virus (FeLV):* Another serious illness, this is a retrovirus that is transferred from cat to cat. It can be fatal for a cat that has contracted the illness.

- *Bordetella:* Bordetella is usually only given to cats that will be boarded or ones that will attend shows. It is an illness commonly known as kennel cough and it can be quite serious if a cat contracts the illness.

Not all of the vaccines are necessary for every cat and an indoor Siberian Cat that lives in a single cat family will usually only need the core vaccines.

c) Vaccine Schedule

Before you get any vaccine for your kitten or Siberian Cat, it is important to speak with your veterinarian. Discuss the illnesses that are in your area and choose the right non-core and core vaccines for your cat with that information.

Although vaccines will vary from area to area, the chart below will identify when you should have a vaccine administered.

	FHV-1/FCV/FPV	RABIES	FIV	FELV	REVOLUTION
7 WEEKS	X				X
9 WEEKS					X
11 WEEKS					X
12 WEEKS	X		X	X	
16 WEEKS	X	X	X	X	
1 YEAR	X	X	X	X	
YEARLY	X	X	X	X	X

5. Common Diseases in Siberian Cats

Now that we have gone over all of the vaccines and health issues that you will deal with as a cat owner, it is time to go over the various diseases that are commonly seen in Siberian Cats.

It is important to note, however, that Siberian Cats are a hardy breed and are not susceptible to a large number of inherent diseases.

a) Feline Lower Urinary Tract Disease

Also known as FLUTD, feline lower urinary tract infection is a very common occurrence in Siberian Cats. The main reason for this is due to the fact that Siberian Cats carry the condition and it is inherited from the parents.

Feline lower urinary tract disease is a condition that causes a series of different conditions including kidney stones, urinary tract infections and blockages. It does not have a high mortality rate.

Symptoms:

The symptoms of feline lower urinary tract disease are very easy to spot if you are paying attention to the cat's litter box and his behaviour. Symptoms include:

* Straining to urinate
* Licking of the urinary opening
* Bloody Urine
* Urinating in unusual paces

Cause:

As I have mentioned, feline lower urinary tract disease is a hereditary disease for Siberian Cats, however, it can occur due to several different factors including idiopathic cystitis, bladder stones, urinary infections, cancers and kidney failure.

A poor diet as well as stress can also be attributed as the cause of feline lower urinary tract disease.

Treatment:

Treatment of the feline lower urinary tract disease varies depending on the age of the Siberian Cat and also on the cause of the disease.

b) Hereditary Cancer

While the occurrence of cancer in cats is fairly low, the risk of a Siberian Cat developing cancer is actually quite high for the breed. There are a range of different cancers that you can see, however, it is more commonly seen in solid white Siberian Cats.

With other colours in the breed, there have been very few cases of cancers and the cancers that do occur are usually due to secondary causes and are not hereditary.

Symptoms:

Symptoms for hereditary cancers vary depending on the type of cancer that the cat contracts. Symptoms can include:

* Tumours
* Lethargy
* Sores
* Decreased appetite
* Difficulty swallowing
* Changes in bowel movements
* Decreased urination
* Coughing and Wheezing
* Stiffness
* Unexplained bleeding or discharge

Cause:

As I have mentioned, causes of hereditary cancer in Siberian Cats is due to genetics. Cats, particularly white Siberian Cats, carry the cancer gene.

Treatment:

Treatment varies depending on the type of cancer that it is. It can include medication, surgery, chemotherapy or a combination of all of the treatment options.

c) Hypertrophic Cardiomyopathy

Hypertrophic Cardiomyopathy, which is commonly known as HCM, is a disease that affects the heart of the cat. It is actually very common in all breeds of cats and it has a high occurrence in Siberian Cats.

Symptoms:

With this disease, symptoms are not always seen early on, however, they are seen as the disease progresses. Some symptoms that you see are:

* Loss of appetite
* Weight loss
* Heart Murmur
* Lethargy
* Increased heart rate
* Increased respiratory rate
* Sudden death

The disease often affects cats between the ages of 1 to 5 years, however, it has been seen in kittens as young as 3 months of age and in senior cats around the age of 10.

Cause:

The cause of hypertrophic cardiomyopathy is not known and it is believed to be a genetic condition. When it occurs, the walls of the ventricles thicken and scar tissue begins to replace the muscle fibres of the heart. As this occurs, the heart weakens and becomes less elastic.

Treatment:

Treatment of hypertrophic cardiomyopathy is usually through prevention and drug intervention. Many times, a drug is given to relax the heart and most cats will need to take a cardiovascular drug. Another treatment option is daily aspirin, however, this should only be given at the recommendations of a veterinarian.

Finally, the cat should be a on a strict low-salt diet. The disease is progressive and the condition will continue to get worse without proper care and maintenance of your Siberian Cat.

d) Gum Disease

The final disease that is commonly seen in Siberian Cats is gum disease. This disease creates a deterioration of the gum, which leads to the cat having to have his teeth removed.

Symptoms:

There are several symptoms of gum disease and it often begins with an inflammation around a tooth. As it becomes more advanced, you may see:

* Bleeding gums
* Separation of the gum and tooth
* Discomfort when eating
* Loss of appetite
* Gum tissue receding

Cause:

The cause of gum disease can be due to bacteria but in the case of Siberian Cats, it is usually an inherited disease.

Treatment:

Treatment varies depending on the stage at which it occurs. Often, it is done through cleanings and applying an antibacterial gel to the gums. It can also be treated with surgery and by removing the teeth.

One of the best ways to prevent gum disease in your Siberian Cat is to make teeth brushing a daily habit.

Chapter 11. Breeding your Siberian Cat

So you are interested in breeding your cat. Before you do, be prepared for a big responsibility. Raising a litter of kittens can be very difficult and they should stay with you until they are at least 10 weeks of age, although it is better if they wait until they are 12 weeks old.

That being said, breeding has many pros and cons. Cats are heavily overpopulated and hundreds of thousands of cats wind up in shelters on a yearly basis. Bringing a litter into the world makes you responsible for those cats so make sure you do your research before you breed. In addition, follow up with the homes you have placed your kittens in.

Before I go into breeding, I want to stress that this is a summary of breeding. The actual act of breeding your cat and raising kittens is something that could take up an entire book so I have just gone over the general information.

If you are interested in breeding Siberian Cats in a serious manner, I recommend that you find a Siberian Cat mentor to help you learn everything you need to know about breeding.

1. Choosing your Breeding Stock

The first thing that you should do if you would like to breed your Siberian Cat is to choose your breeding stock. This is very important in ensuring that you get the desired look and temperaments in your kittens.

Firstly, read the breed standard. Make sure that the Siberian Cats that you are raising meet the breed standard. While you are not

101

going to have a cat that is perfect, you want to make sure that both cats are as close to the breed standard as possible.

In addition, if there is a trait that is not breed standard, do not breed two cats with the same trait. This will only increase the likelihood of the undesirable trait being passed on to the kittens.

If both of the cats are excellent representations of the Siberian Cat breed standard, it is still not enough to breed them. Make sure you check their pedigrees to avoid inbreeding the cats. While it can be done, it should only be done by experts. Breeding too closely related can cause several health problems.

Another area that you need to be sure to check is the health of the cats. If the Siberian Cats have any diseases or a history of disease in their families, avoid using that cat for your breeding program. There are several diseases that are inherent and you should avoid using cats that have the disease.

Finally, use cats that are registered. While there are purebred Siberian Cats out there, to prevent overpopulation with Siberian Cats, it is important to choose parents that are registered.

2. The Siberian Cat Female

Although I could go over males, in this chapter, I am not going to as we want to focus on the female and the actual pregnancy. Male cats should be healthy, as I have mentioned and should be an excellent specimen of the Siberian Cat. Once you have the male, it is simply a matter of breeding the animals.

The female cat should also be healthy and while both animals should have a veterinary exam and health tests done, this is imperative for your female Siberian Cat.

Before you breed your cat, it is important that you take the cat to the veterinarian's office for a physical. The vet should check on the overall health of the cat.

The Siberian Cat should also be checked for intestinal parasites. Vaccinations should be given prior to breeding and if the Siberian Cat has not had the feline rhinotracheitis booster in the last 6 months it should be given it. Feline panleukopenia and feline leukemia vaccinations should also be given if the female has not received it in the last 2 years.

Once your female cat has been given a clean bill of health and is updated with her vaccinations, you can breed her.

a) When to Breed

One question that is commonly asked with cats is when you can breed the female. The answer is that the female should be over the age of 1. In addition, a female cat should never be bred on the first heat as this can result in health risks for your female.

With heats, a cat will often enter her first heat when she is roughly 6 months of age or about 5 pounds in size. The heat lasts 4 to 7 days and a cat will have several heats through the year.

In general, cats tend to be seasonal animals with their heats occurring most frequently in fall and spring. However, that being said, a female cat will go into heat every 6 to 12 weeks. It is important to note that some cats go into heat more frequently than every 6 weeks.

When a female cat is ready to be bred, she begins to show the behaviours associated with being on heat. She will:

* Become very vocal.

* Try to escape the house to get outside.

* Become very playful and will often roll around on the floor.

* Stand with her back arched and her tail straight up when she is touched. Her back legs will stiffen as well.

* Will rub against you and the furniture.

While they are in heat, a female cat can be bred to more than one male over her heat cycle and this can lead to the kittens in the litter having multiple fathers.

If you are trying to pair only one male with your female, it is imperative that you keep them segregated from other cats during the breeding period. If you don't, you will end up with several different fathers.

b) Breeding

As I mentioned, breeding will take place over the course of 4 to 7 days and it can occur with more than one male. Breeding can be quite traumatic for first time cat breeders since the penis of the male has small barbs on them, which are known as penile spines. These spines scratch the walls of the female's vagina during mating and the female will often cry out during mating due to this.

It is unclear as to why a male cat has penile spines; however, some studies have indicated that it may cause ovulation.

c) Pregnancy

After breeding occurs, and, in the case of most Siberian Cats, several breedings will occur, the female will often become pregnant. For cats, the average length of pregnancy is roughly 64 days, however, it can be anywhere between 64 and 67 days.

During pregnancy, the proper care of your Siberian Cat is imperative. Good nutrition will enable the kittens to grow well in the womb and will help the mother, or queen as female cats are called, overcome the drain that pregnancy and nursing a litter can take on their health.

With feeding, you should maintain her regular feeding habits for the first 6 weeks of the pregnancy. Don't give her anything extra as you do not want her to become obese, which can have health risks during delivery.

Once she reaches 6 weeks of pregnancy, start increasing the amount of food that she is eating. A good rule of thumb is to give her 25% more food from 6 weeks on and to continue increasing it as she needs. In addition, switch to a kitten food for the mom so she gets enough calcium in her diet.

Also, as the pregnancy progresses, feed her smaller meals each time and increase the number of times that she eats in the day. Pregnant cats have a difficult time eating big meals the closer they get to the delivery date since the kittens are resting on their internal organs.

Make sure that she has plenty of water and don't discourage her from her daily exercise. Cats will behave in much the same way as they did prior to pregnancy and exercise will help maintain her health.

After the kittens are born, you will need to continue increasing the amount of food that she eats for the first 30 days. The reason for this is because it takes a lot of energy to nurse the kittens. By the time the kittens are weaned, the mother should be eating 2 to 4 times her pre-pregnancy quantities.

d) The Delivery

After your cat has been pregnant for 62 to 67 days, she will go into labour. Before she does, it is important to be prepared for it. Set up a room that is warm and does not have any drafts. You want a floor that can be cleaned easily.

Set up the room with a litter box as well as her food and water; make sure to keep the food and litter box separated. Prepare a bed in one area of the room. I find the best bed to use is a laundry basin that has been lined with clean towels.

Introduce her to the bed well before she is due for delivery so she becomes accustomed to the bed and looks for it when she goes into labour. One of the best things to do is to sit beside the bed and pet her while she is in it. Give her plenty of treats during the time so she begins to view the bed as a good place.

Regardless of how accustomed your Siberian Cat gets to her bed, there is a big chance that she will have her kittens outside of the bed. If this happens, don't stress, simply allow her to have her kittens and then move them all to your designated bed when she is done delivering.

At the time of delivery, you may find that she is more restless than she normally is. She may also try to escape outside so it is important to keep her in a safe area in the home.

When she goes into labour, it is best to simply allow her to do things on her own. While it may be comforting to you to get involved and try to comfort her, it can actually cause stress, which can lead to her abandoning the kittens.

Instead, give her some space and watch from a distance. If you see any signs that she is in distress, intervene at the discretion of your vet. If there aren't any signs, just enjoy the kittens and the labour process. It will take a few hours but goes quite quickly.

When the delivery is done and the mom has settled down enough, you can move her to her bed and let her relax with her kittens. If you find the room is cold, place a heating pad under the bottom of the basket, make sure you wrap it in towels for safety. Keep it to one half so the kittens can move away from the heat to prevent overheating.

3. The Siberian Cat Kitten

When it comes to the care of a newborn kitten, there really isn't a lot that you need to do. Siberian Cats are excellent mothers and they will see to the needs of their kittens from day one.

At birth, most kittens will weigh between 85 to 120 grams. It is important to weigh them daily during the first two weeks to ensure that they are growing. By the end of the 2nd week of life, their weight should be double what it was at birth. On average, kittens will gain about 10 grams every day; however, don't be alarmed if there are a few days where they haven't gained as many kittens grow in growth spurts.

When they are born, a kitten's eyes should be closed and the ears will be folded and they cannot see or hear. By 14 days of age, their eyes should open and they will begin to move around a bit on their legs, although they will be very shaky.

At 3 weeks of age, their ears should be open and should be standing erect. The kitten should be walking around well and should be starting to develop unique personality traits.

Before 3 weeks of age, the kittens will be nursing from their mother but at 3 to 4 weeks of age, you can begin introducing wet food for the kittens. This will aid in weaning and will take some of the stress off of the mother.

At 6 to 8 weeks of age, the kittens should be completely weaned and should no longer be nursing from their mum. They should be eating solids and should be very secure with walking.

When your kittens reach 7 weeks old, they should be seen by a veterinarian and should have their first set of shots. Their second set of shots should be given at 9 weeks of age.

As they grow, it is important to introduce them to the litter box, read the chapter on litter training to learn more. Also, it is important to handle them daily and to socialize them to a range of stimuli.

Finally, the kittens are ready for their new homes at 10 to 12 weeks of age. 12 weeks is the ideal but they can go to their new homes at 10 weeks.

Raising kittens can be wonderful but it is important to do it properly and learn as much as you can before you breed your cat.

Chapter 12. Common Terms

So you are interested in owning a Siberian Cat. Well, if you want to be a true Siberian Cat lover, you should become confident with some of the terms that are used by cat lovers around the world.

- *Alter:* To neuter or spay a cat to prevent it from reproducing offspring.

- *Bloodline:* Refers to the pedigree or family tree of the cat.

- *Breeder:* A person who breeds two animals and aids in the raising of the young of those animals.

- *Bridge:* The bony ridge on the top of the nose.

- *Britches:* When there is longer hair on the top of the back legs, creating a pant-like look to the hair.

- *Brush:* Referring to a bushy tail.

- *Buff:* The act of the cat rubbing its face on something.

- *Caregiver:* A person who owns a cat as a pet.

- *Carnivore:* An animal that eats meat as its primary food source. Cats are carnivores.

- *Castrate:* Removing the testicles of a male cat through a surgical procedure. Also known as neutering.

- *Cat Candy:* A common term that refers to cat treats.

- *Cat Collector:* A person who owns and hoards a large number of cats. Also known as a cat hoarder.

- *Cat Fancy:* A term referring to a group of people who are members of a cat association.

- *Clowder:* A term referring to a group of cats.

- *Crossbreed: 1.* The act of breeding two cats together from different breeds. *2.* The offspring that are produced by the mating of two cats from different breeds.

- *Curl:* Refers to a sleeping position commonly seen in cats where the cat will sleep with its head resting on its forelegs.

- *Domestic:* A term that is used to describe any breed of cat that has adapted to humans so there is a genetic predisposition to tameness.

- *Feline Panleukopenia:* A serious viral infection.

- *Ex- Feral:* Referring to a cat that has been tamed after being wild.

- *Feral:* A cat that is wild. This could be due to being born in the wild or an ex-domestic cat that has reverted back to being wild.

- *Fixing:* To neuter or spay a cat to prevent it from reproducing offspring.

- *Flake Out:* A term that refers to the way a cat lies on its side or belly in a stretched pose.

- *Full Tom:* An adult male cat that has not been neutered.

- *Half Pedigree:* Also known as a moggy, it is a term used to describe a cat that has only one pedigreed parent.

- *Herbivore:* An animal that primarily eats vegetation and plants as its main food source.

- *Hissed Off:* A term referring to an annoyed cat that has begun hissing.

- *House Cat:* A cat that does not go outside and won't leave the house.

- *Hybrid:* Also known as a cross breed, the offspring that are produced by the mating of two cats from different breeds.

-*Inbreeding:* The act of mating two cats that are closely related such as sibling to sibling or father to daughter in the attempt to strengthen certain traits in the cat.

- *Intact:* A term referring to a cat that has not been spayed or neutered. This term can be used for males or females.

- *Kindle:* Referring to a group of kittens.

- *Kitten:* The offspring of a cat, it usually refers to a cat that is under the age of 6 months of age.

- *Litter:* A group of kittens that are born to one female

- *Moggy:* Also known as a half pedigree, it is a term used to describe a cat that has only one pedigreed parent.

- *Mutt Cat:* Also known as mixed breed, it is a cat that has several different breeds in its pedigree.

- *Neuter:* Removing the testicles of a male cat through a surgical procedure to prevent reproduction. Also known as castration, it can only be done on male cats.

- *Omnivore:* An animal that eats both plants and meat.

- *Outbreeding:* Breeding cats of the same breed but from different pedigrees. The opposite of inbreeding.

- *Outcrossing:* Breeding one breed of cat to a different breed to produce new traits or improve on developed traits.

- *Pedigree: 1.* Refers to the family tree of the cat. *2.* A cat belonging to a particular breed.

- *Purebred:* A cat that only has one breed in its family tree. All members of its family tree are the same breed as it with no outcrossing.

- *Queen:* A term used to describe an unspayed female cat.

- *Scruff:* The back of the cat's neck where the loose skin is.

- *Scruffing:* A form of discipline.

- *Semi-Feral:* A cat that has lived in a feral state but will experience some contact with humans. Also known as half wild.

- *Spay:* The surgical removal of the ovaries and womb in a cat to prevent reproduction. Also known as an ovario-hysterectomy.

- *Sterilise:* To neuter or spay a cat to prevent it from reproducing offspring.

- *Stray:* A domestic cat that has no owner.

- *Stropping:* The term that refers to a cat sharpening its claws.

- *Teaser Tom:* A neutered male that continues to behave like an unneutered male cat.

- *Tom:* An adult male cat that has not been neutered.

- *Trait:* Referring to a physical or temperament characteristic that can be inherited.

- *Unaltered:* A cat that has not been neutered or spayed.

- *Wild:* A cat that is feral. This could be due to being born in the wild or an ex-domestic cat that has reverted back to being feral.

CPSIA information can be obtained
at www.ICGtesting.com
Printed in the USA
BVHW061116260820
587355BV00003B/167

9 781909 151703